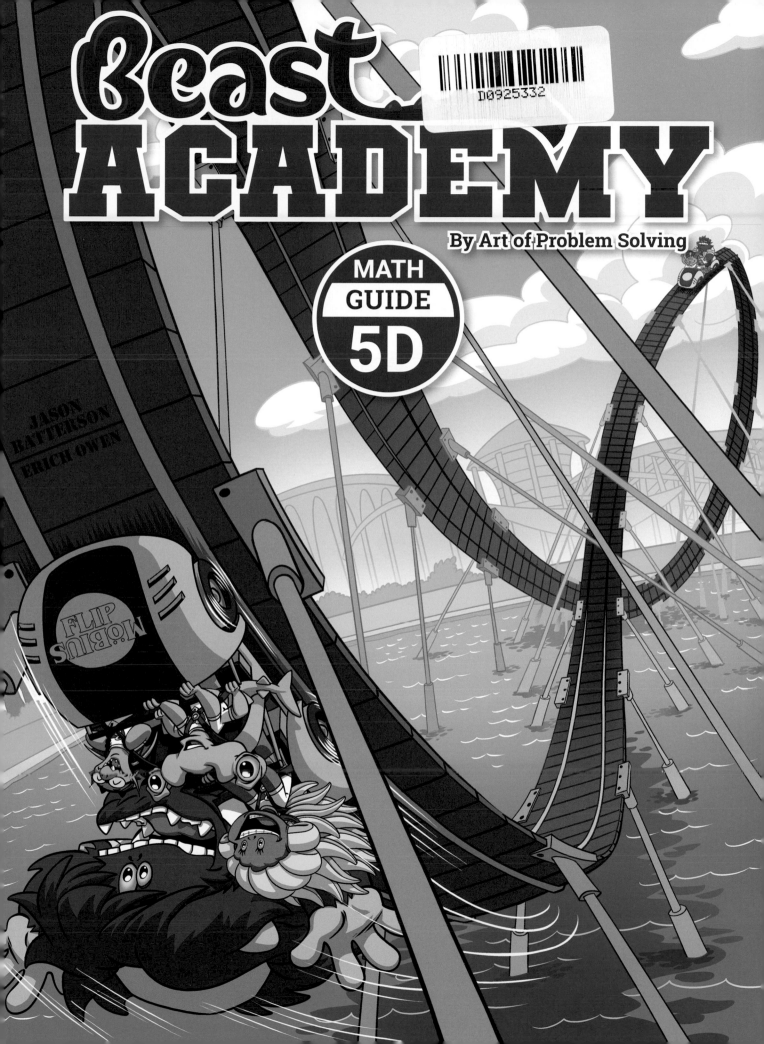

Published by: AoPS Incorporated
                  10865 Rancho Bernardo Rd Ste 100
                  San Diego, CA 92127-2102
                  info@BeastAcademy.com

ISBN: 978-1-934124-66-6

Written by Jason Batterson
Illustrated by Erich Owen
Additional Illustrations by Paul Cox
Colored by Greta Selman

Visit the Beast Academy website at BeastAcademy.com.
Visit the Art of Problem Solving website at artofproblemsolving.com.
Printed in the United States of America.
2021 Printing.

Become a Math Beast!
For additional books,
printables, and more, visit

BeastAcademy.com

This is Guide 5D in a four-book series:

Guide 5A
Chapter 1: 3D Solids
Chapter 2: Integers
Chapter 3: Expressions & Equations

Guide 5B
Chapter 4: Statistics
Chapter 5: Factors & Multiples
Chapter 6: Fractions

Guide 5C
Chapter 7: Sequences
Chapter 8: Ratios & Rates
Chapter 9: Decimals

Guide 5D
Chapter 10: Percents
Chapter 11: Square Roots
Chapter 12: Exponents

Contents:

Characters 6

How to Use This Book 8

Chapter 10: Percents 12

Percents & Fractions 14

Percents & Decimals 19

Percent of a Number 24

Finding Percents 28

Proportions 33

Chapter 11: Square Roots 40

Square Roots 42

Lizzie's Notes 47

Estimation 48

More or Less 55

Tricky Square Roots 56

The Pythagorean Theorem 64

Chapter 12: Exponents 72

Exponents 74

Negative Exponents 80

Pneumatube 84

The WMOC 90

Channel 5 92

The Finals 93

Index 110

Lizzie
"The BOOkwOrm"
can name every
dragOn species
On
Beast Island
(alphabetically)

Alex
"The Executive"
Plans tO run fOr
city cOmptrOller
when he's Old enOugh
fOr public Office

Winnie
"The Firecracker"   Feisty!
GrOws 50 times
her Original size when angry!
(nOt really, but it's fun
to draw her that way)

GrOgg (me)
"The ^least common DenOminatOr"

ALter EgO:
FractiOn JacksOn!

Mr. Wriggles

kraken
shop Teacher

Favorite pattern?
Arrrrrgyle

Favorite holiday?
Arrrrrbor Day

Favorite element?
~~Arrrrrrgon~~
GOld

FiOna
Math Team cOach

DOnated her hair to
"Braids fOr Mermaids"
this summer

PrOfessOr GrOk
Math Lab
(full Of bOOby traps)

cOnstantly
captured by

"calamitOus clOd"

Ms. Q.
Math Teacher

Spends a lOt
Of time
with Mr. **A.**

R&G
campus Maintenance
Engineer(s?)

Let me ride
in their
gOlf cart
Once!

Sgt. ROte →
Gym Teacher

can bench press
three times
his Own bOdyweight!
(4lbs.)

The Headmaster
How to use this book

Welcome to Beast Academy!

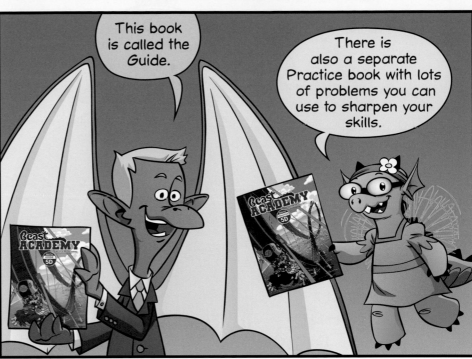

This book is called the Guide.

There is also a separate Practice book with lots of problems you can use to sharpen your skills.

The Guide is written like a comic book.

In a comic book, whatever I say shows up in these bubbles. They're called comic balloons.

Here's one!

Each character has a different balloon color. This makes it easy to tell who is talking.

My balloons are purple!

The story is told in panels.

Panels usually have a rectangular frame around them...

...like this one.

If you've gotten this far, you probably know a little bit about how to read a comic book.

You read a comic book the same way you read any other book... from left to right and from top to bottom.

But sometimes, panels don't have frames...

...like the open panel I'm in now.

On each page, start in the top left panel.

Go to the right, then down.

Read all of the balloons in each panel from left to right and top to bottom before moving to the next panel.

At first, you may need to think about which balloon to read next.

Like when lots of characters are talking.

Or when a character speaks more than once.

Right! And sometimes several balloons get connected.

With a little practice, reading comics becomes natural.

How many panels are on this page?

9

Practice: Pages 6, 36, and 64.

Contents: Chapter 10

See page 6 in the Practice book for a recommended reading/practice sequence for Chapter 10.

Percents & Fractions   14
How could you write $\frac{1}{6}$ as a percent?

Percents & Decimals   19
How do you write 0.0046 as a percent?

Percent of a Number   24
How much is 6% of $1,050?

Finding Percents   28
What percent of 4 is 5?

Proportions   33
What happens when you mix just the right amount of lemon juice with 15 milliliters of hippopotamoose drool?
(Do not try this at home.)

Chapter 10: Percents

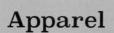

Ms. Q.
Percents & Fractions

New vest, Alex?

Yep.

90 percent of the reviewers at SuaveShark.com recommend it.

THE SYMBOL FOR PERCENT IS %. WE USUALLY WRITE "90 PERCENT" AS 90%.

What does that mean?

Percent means "out of 100."

So, 90% means 90 out of 100.

So, there were 100 reviewers, and 90 of them recommended your vest?

Not necessarily.

90% doesn't tell us how many reviewers there were...

...just what fraction of the reviewers liked my vest.

14

To convert a percent to a fraction, we just write the number over 100 and simplify.

$6\% = \frac{6}{100} = \frac{3}{50}.$

$$6\% = \frac{6}{100}$$
$$= \frac{3}{50}$$

155% is $\frac{155}{100}$...

...which simplifies to $\frac{31}{20}$.

$$155\% = \frac{155}{100}$$
$$= \frac{31}{20}$$

0.3% is $\frac{0.3}{100}$.

But, we don't want a decimal in our fraction.

We can get rid of the decimal by multiplying by 10 on top and bottom.

So, 0.3% is $\frac{3}{1,000}$.

$$0.3\% = \frac{0.3}{100} \overset{\cdot 10}{\underset{\cdot 10}{=}} \frac{3}{1,000}$$

Good.

We can also write any fraction as a percent.

How can we write each of these fractions as a percent?

$$\frac{63}{100} \qquad \frac{4}{5} \qquad \frac{1}{6}$$

Try all three.

16

Since $\frac{63}{100}$ already has 100 in its denominator, it's easy to write as a percent.

$\frac{63}{100}$ equals 63%.

$$\frac{63}{100} = 63\%$$

We can convert $\frac{4}{5}$ into a fraction with denominator 100.

$\frac{4}{5} = \frac{80}{100}$, which is 80%.

$$\frac{4}{5} = \frac{80}{100} = 80\%$$

$\cdot 20$

$\cdot 20$

Turning $\frac{1}{6}$ into a fraction with denominator 100 is harder.

There isn't an integer we can multiply 6 by to get 100.

But, we can set up an equation and solve for x.

$$\frac{1}{6} = \frac{x}{100}$$

Suave Shark

90% customer satisfaction

To solve for x, we multiply both sides of the equation by 100.

$$\frac{1}{6} \cdot 100 = \frac{x}{100} \cdot 100$$

$\frac{100}{6} = x$.

$$\frac{100}{6} = x$$

As a mixed number, $\frac{100}{6} = \frac{50}{3}$, or $16\frac{2}{3}$.

$$16\frac{2}{3} = x$$

35% is $\frac{35}{100}$, which is 0.35, sir!

35%

$= \frac{35}{100}$

$= 0.35$

430% is $\frac{430}{100}$, or $4\frac{30}{100}$. That's $4\frac{3}{10}$, or 4.3, sir!

430%

$= \frac{430}{100}$

$= 4\frac{30}{100}$

$= 4\frac{3}{10}$

$= 4.3$

$$0.05\% = \frac{0.05}{100} = \frac{5}{10{,}000} = 0.0005$$

$\cdot 100$

$\cdot 100$

0.05% is $\frac{0.05}{100}$, which is $\frac{5}{10{,}000}$.

To write $\frac{5}{10{,}000}$ as a decimal, we put a 5 in the 10,000ths place, sir! 0.05%=0.0005.

Affirmative.

If you can convert a percent to a decimal, you can convert a decimal to a percent.

Convert each of these decimals to a percent.

0.08

0.4

0.00246

Try all three.

20

0.08

$$= \frac{8}{100}$$

$$= 8\%$$

0.08 is $\frac{8}{100}$, which is 8%, sir!

0.4 is 0.40, or $\frac{40}{100}$.

0.40

$$= \frac{40}{100}$$

$$= 40\%$$

That's 40%, sir!

Next, we need to find out what number over 100 equals 0.00246.

$$0.00246 = \frac{x}{100}$$

We can write an equation.

$$0.00246 \cdot 100 = \frac{x}{100} \cdot 100$$

$$0.246 = x$$

Multiplying both sides of the equation by 100, we get $x = 0.246$.

$$0.00246 = \frac{0.246}{100} = 0.246\%$$

So, 0.00246 equals 0.246 over 100...

...which means 0.00246 is 0.246%, sir.

Good work, hammerhead. Who sees a pattern in these conversions?

Notice any patterns?

When we converted 0.08, 0.4, and 0.00246 to percents...

...we got 8%, 40%, and 0.246%.

We just moved the decimal point two places to the right and added a percent sign, sir.

$$0.08 = 8\%$$
$$0.4 = 40\%$$
$$0.00246 = 0.246\%$$

Will that work for converting any decimal to a percent?

Sir, yes, sir!

Why is that, Pinkie?

To convert any decimal to a percent, we can multiply the decimal by 100.

$$0.4 \cdot 100 = \frac{x}{100} \cdot 100$$
$$40 = x$$

Multiplying a decimal by 100 shifts its decimal point two places to the right.

And then we write a percent sign at the end, sir!

$$0.4 = 40\%$$

Well done.

Is there a similar method we can use to convert any percent to a decimal?

Can you find a shortcut for converting percents to decimals?

22

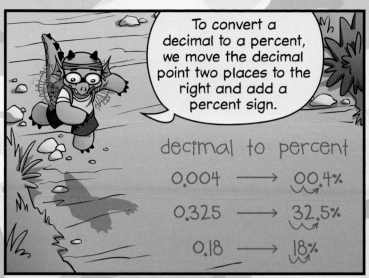

How do we find a percent of a number?

We can find a *fraction* of a number just by multiplying the fraction by the number.

So, if we convert the percent into a fraction, we can multiply.

15% is $\frac{15}{100}$.

So, 15% of $6,000 is $\frac{15}{100} \cdot 6{,}000$ dollars.

$$15\% \text{ of } \$6{,}000$$
$$= \frac{15}{100} \times 6{,}000$$
$$= \frac{15 \times 6{,}000}{100}$$
$$= 15 \times \frac{6{,}000}{100}$$
$$= 15 \times 60$$
$$= 900$$

That's $900.

You could also start by changing the percent to a decimal, then multiplying.

$$15\% \text{ of } \$6{,}000$$
$$= 0.15 \times 6{,}000$$
$$= (15 \times 0.01) \times (6 \times 1{,}000)$$
$$= (15 \times 6) \times (0.01 \times 1{,}000)$$
$$= 90 \times 10$$
$$= 900$$

15% is 0.15. So, 15% of $6,000 is 0.15 · 6,000 dollars.

Still $900.

15% of $6,000 is easy enough to compute in my head.

How'd you do it, lass?

25

I know 10% is $\frac{1}{10}$, and one tenth of $6,000 is $600.

5% of $6,000 is half of 10% of $6,000.

That's $300.

And 15% of $6,000 is 10% of $6,000 plus 5% of $6,000. That's $600+$300=$900.

10% of $6,000 = $600

5% of $6,000 = $300

15% of $6,000 = $900

Aye. There be many ways to compute a percent of a number.

'Tis one o' the reasons percents be so commonly used.

Whoa. The tax on spiralac feathers is only 6%!

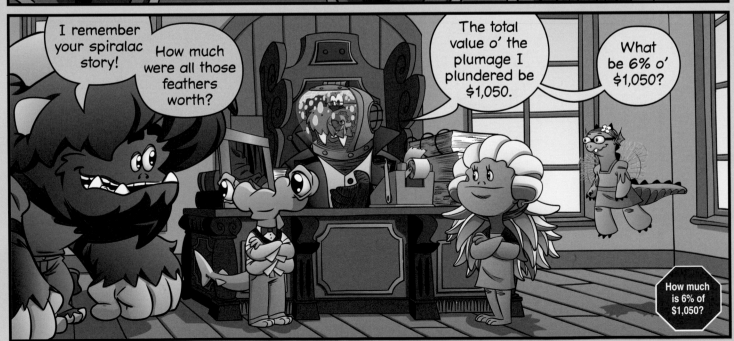

I remember your spiralac story!

How much were all those feathers worth?

The total value o' the plumage I plundered be $1,050.

What be 6% o' $1,050?

How much is 6% of $1,050?

26

6% is $\frac{6}{100}$.

So, 6% of $1,050 is $\frac{6}{100} \cdot 1,050$ dollars.

$$\frac{6}{100} \times 1,050$$
$$= \frac{6 \times 1,050}{100}$$
$$= \frac{6,300}{100}$$
$$= 63$$

That's $63.

I converted 6% to a decimal and multiplied.

$$1,050 \times 0.06$$
$$= 1,050 \times 6 \times 0.01$$
$$= 6,300 \times 0.01$$
$$= 63$$

I figured that 6% of $100 is $6.

So, 6% of $1,000 is $60, and 6% of $50 is $3.

6% OF $100 = $6
6% OF $1,000 = $60
6% OF $50 = $3
6% OF $1,050 = $63

That means 6% of $1,050 is 60+3=63 dollars.

I found 6% of $1,050 in my head, too.

First, I found 1% of $1,050. Then, I multiplied by 6 to find 6% of $1,050.

1% of 1,050 is 0.01·$1,050=$10.50, so 6% of $1,050 is 6·$10.50=$63.

1% OF $1,050 = $10.50
6% OF $1,050 = 6 × $10.50 = $63

Practice: Pages 16-23

Well done, little buccaneers. Computin' the percents be the easy part.

It's all these forms that be givin' me headaches.

Scooch over. I've been helping my parents prepare their taxes since I was 6!

Call me "Kindling."

Huh?

Because I'm on fire!

What percent of your shots have you made?

I've made 9 out of 15 shots.

What percent is that?

What percent of 15 is 9?

28

$$\frac{9}{15} = \frac{x}{100}$$

$$\frac{900}{15} = x$$

$$60 = x$$

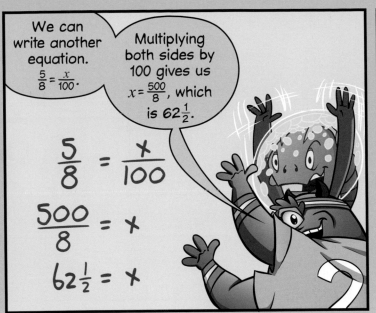

A PROPORTION IS AN EQUATION SHOWING THAT TWO RATIOS ARE EQUAL.
WE LEARNED ABOUT PROPORTIONS AND HOW TO SOLVE THEM IN CHAPTER 8 OF BEAST ACADEMY 5C.

There are lots of ways to solve for x.

I simplified $\frac{15}{100}$ to $\frac{3}{20}$. Then, I noticed that $\frac{3}{20} = \frac{6}{40}$. So, $x = 40$.

So, the whole mixture is **40** milliliters.

$$\frac{6}{x} = \frac{15}{100}$$

$$\frac{6}{x} = \frac{3}{20}$$

$$\frac{6}{40} = \frac{3}{20}$$

Quite right. Watch what happens when we add a drop of the ink mixture to a small piece of construction paper.

Goggles on, little monsters!

Whoa!

Whiiirrooosh!

Let's try another mixture.

How many milliliters of lemon juice must be added to 15 milliliters of hippopotamoose drool to make a mixture that is 4% hippopotamoose drool?

Ew.

GAZELLEPHANT MUCUS

MAMBAT VENOM

RATTLESNAIL SLIME

HIPPOPOTAMOOSE DROOL

ANACONDOR TEARS

SALAMANATEE SALIVA

PORCUPUMA SWEAT

Try it.

If we figure out how many milliliters there are in the **whole** mixture, we can figure out how many milliliters of lemon juice to add.

We just need to figure out what number 15 is 4% of.

If y is the total number of milliliters in the mixture...

$$\text{drool} \longrightarrow \dfrac{15}{y} = \dfrac{4}{100} \longleftarrow \text{total}$$

...then 15 out of y milliliters is 4% of the total mixture. So, we have $\dfrac{15}{y} = \dfrac{4}{100}$.

Multiplying both sides of the equation by $100y$ gives us $1{,}500 = 4y$.

Then, dividing both sides by 4 gives us $375 = y$.

So, the whole mixture is 375 milliliters.

$$\dfrac{15}{\cancel{y}} \cdot 100\cancel{y} = \dfrac{4}{\cancel{100}} \cdot \cancel{100}\,y$$
$$1{,}500 = 4y$$
$$375 = y$$

And since there are 15 mL of drool in the mixture, the other $375 - 15 = 360$ mL is lemon juice.

Well done. Watch what happens when we add 360 mL of lemon juice to 15 mL of hippopotamoose drool.

Bwah Hah Hah! Professor Grok is gone! I've abducted your educator! It's time for something much more diabolically difficult!

Solving such simple percent proportions is preposterously pedestrian.

To aid your educator's escape, you must ponder this perplexing percent proportion.

How many milliliters of rattlesnail slime must be mixed into 30 milliliters of porcupuma perspiration to produce a preparation that is precisely 20 percent slime?

Only the specific slime solution will secure the safety of your schoolteacher.

An incorrect concoction will cause...

...*Cataclysmic Chemical Combustion!*

What just happened?

We need to figure out how much rattlesnail slime to mix with 30 mL of porcupuma sweat to make a mixture that is 20% slime.

But, if we mix the wrong amount...

...the whole thing could explode!

Ew.

How much slime?

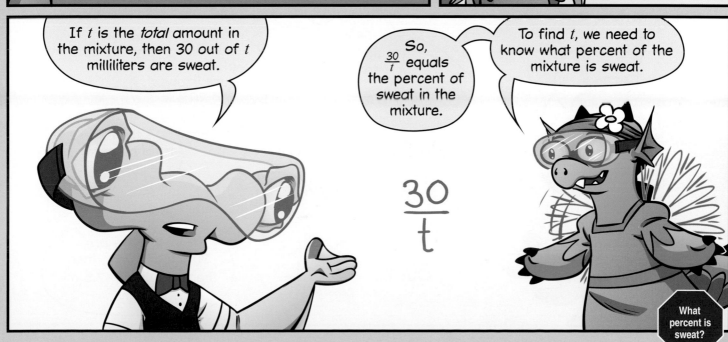

I know! In a mixture of slime and sweat, if 20% is slime...

...then the other **80%** is sweat.

$80\% = \frac{80}{100}$.

So, $\frac{30}{t} = \frac{80}{100}$.

$$\frac{30}{t} = \frac{80}{100}$$

Of course! Solving for t, we get $t = 37\frac{1}{2}$.

So, there are $37\frac{1}{2}$ mL in the whole mixture.

Since 30 mL of the mix is sweat...

...the other $37\frac{1}{2} - 30 = 7\frac{1}{2}$ mL is slime.

$$\frac{30}{\cancel{t}} \cdot 100\cancel{t} = \frac{80}{\cancel{100}} \cdot \cancel{100}t$$
$$3{,}000 = 80t$$
$$\frac{3{,}000}{80} = t$$
$$37\frac{1}{2} = t$$

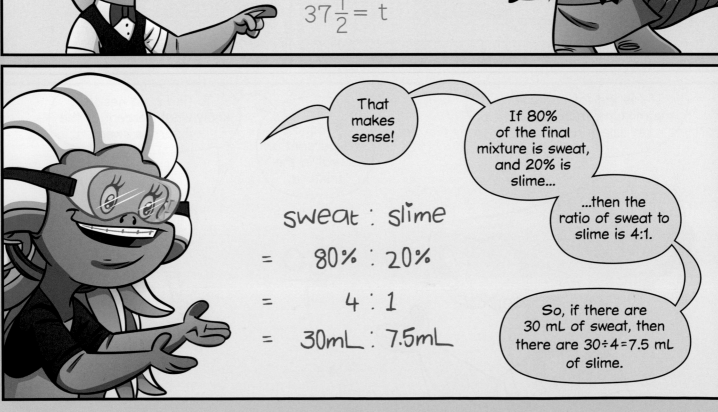

That makes sense!

If 80% of the final mixture is sweat, and 20% is slime...

...then the ratio of sweat to slime is 4:1.

So, if there are 30 mL of sweat, then there are $30 \div 4 = 7.5$ mL of slime.

sweat : slime

= 80% : 20%

= 4 : 1

= 30mL : 7.5mL

Practice: Pages 24-35

Contents: Chapter 11

See page 36 in the Practice book for a recommended reading/practice sequence for Chapter 11.

Square Roots 42
What is the square root of 961?

Lizzie's Notes 47
Can you square 9.5 in your head?

Estimation 48
Does 20 have a square root?

More or Less 55
Is $3\sqrt{3}$ more or less than $2\sqrt{5}$?

Tricky Square Roots 56
How can you find $\sqrt{27 \cdot 12}$ without multiplying $27 \cdot 12$?

The Pythagorean Theorem 64
How long is the hypotenuse of a right triangle whose legs are 3 feet and 5 feet long?

Chapter 11:
Square Roots

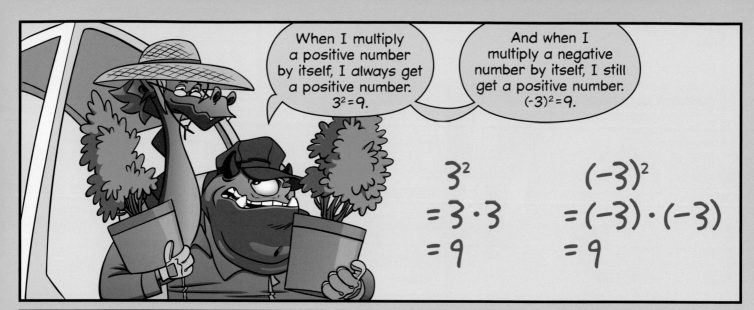

When I multiply a positive number by itself, I always get a positive number. $3^2 = 9$.

And when I multiply a negative number by itself, I still get a positive number. $(-3)^2 = 9$.

$$3^2$$
$$= 3 \cdot 3$$
$$= 9$$

$$(-3)^2$$
$$= (-3) \cdot (-3)$$
$$= 9$$

So, I guess -9 doesn't have a square root.

Since we can't square a number to get a negative result...

...negative numbers don't have square roots.*

*ACTUALLY, THERE ARE SPECIAL NUMBERS WHOSE SQUARES ARE NEGATIVE. MATH BEASTS CALL THEM *IMAGINARY NUMBERS*. AS YOU STUDY MORE MATH, YOU WILL LEARN MORE ABOUT THEM.

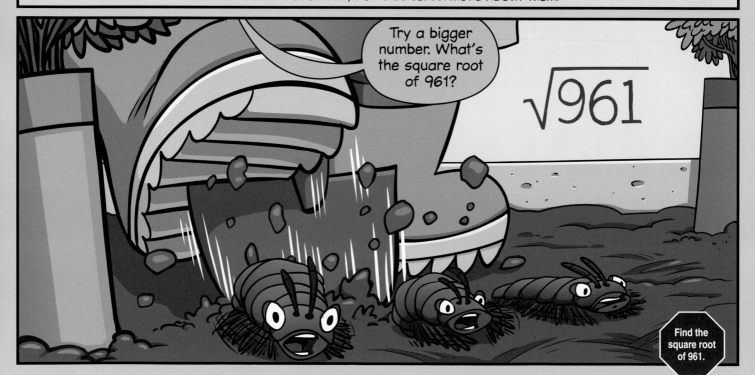

Try a bigger number. What's the square root of 961?

$$\sqrt{961}$$

Find the square root of 961.

$$30^2 = 900 \qquad 35^2 = 1,225$$

$35^2 = 30 \cdot 40 + 25$. REVIEW SQUARING NUMBERS THAT END IN 5 IN BEAST ACADEMY 3B AND ON PAGE 47.

$$31^2 = 30^2 + 30 + 31 = 961$$

$$\sqrt{961} = 31$$

$$\sqrt{0.0121}$$

Try it.

$$11^2 = 121$$

$$1.1^2 = 1.1 \times 1.1 = 1.21$$

$$0.11^2 = 0.11 \times 0.11 = 0.0121$$

$$\sqrt{0.0121} = 0.11$$

RAISING A NUMBER TO THE THIRD POWER (n^3) IS CALLED "CUBING" THE NUMBER. THE **CUBE ROOT** OF A NUMBER IS THE VALUE YOU **CUBE** TO GET THE NUMBER.

Squaring Numbers

 Lizzie

Finding the next square:
To get from 5^2 to 6^2, we add 5 and 6 to 5^2: $5^2+5+6=6^2$.
To get from 30^2 to 31^2, we add 30 and 31 to 30^2: $30^2+30+31=31^2$.

$$6^2 \quad = \quad 5^2+5+6 \qquad\qquad 31^2 \quad = \quad 30^2+30+31$$

= 36

31 1

30^2 30 30

30 1

= 961

Squaring a number that ends in 5:
To square 45, we multiply 40×50 and add 25.
Works for decimals, too! 9.5^2 is 9×10 plus 0.25.

$$45^2 \quad = \quad 40\times50 \;+\; 25 \qquad\qquad 9.5^2 \quad = \quad 9\times10 \;+\; 0.25$$

5
40

40

5
5

5

40   5
40   5 5
50

.5
9

9

.5
.5

.5

9   .5
9   .5 .5
10

= 2,025

= 90.25

We can use a similar diagram to help us square any 2-digit number:

$$67^2 \quad = \quad 60\times60 \;+\; 2\times60\times7 \;+\; 7\times7$$

7
60

60

7
7

60

7
7

60   7
60   7   7

= 3,600 + 840 + 49
= 4,489

√20 is less than √20.25 = 4.5.

So, √20 is closer to 4 than to 5.

√20

√16   √20.25   √25

4   4.5   5

Great!

Grogg, what does that compubot give you for the square root of 20?

√20 is 4.472135954...   ...9995793928...   ...and the digits keep going on and on without any pattern.

√20 = 4.4721359549995793928...

That's right, Grogg. The digits don't repeat regularly.

So, we can't write a decimal that is *exactly* equal to √20...   ...we can only estimate.

How could you estimate √2 to the nearest tenth *without* a compubot?

√2

√20 = 4.472135954 9995793928...

Find √2 to the nearest tenth.

50

√2 is somewhere between √1 = 1 and √4 = 2.

Let's try 1.5. To find out if √2 is more or less than 1.5, we can square 1.5.

Since 1.5² = 2.25...

...1.5 is the square root of 2.25.

$$1.5^2 = 2.25$$
$$1.5 = \sqrt{2.25}$$

So, √2 is between √1 = 1 and √2.25 = 1.5.

Let's try 1.4. Since 14² = 196, 1.4² = 1.96.

So, 1.4 = √1.96.

$$1.4^2 = 1.96$$
$$1.4 = \sqrt{1.96}$$

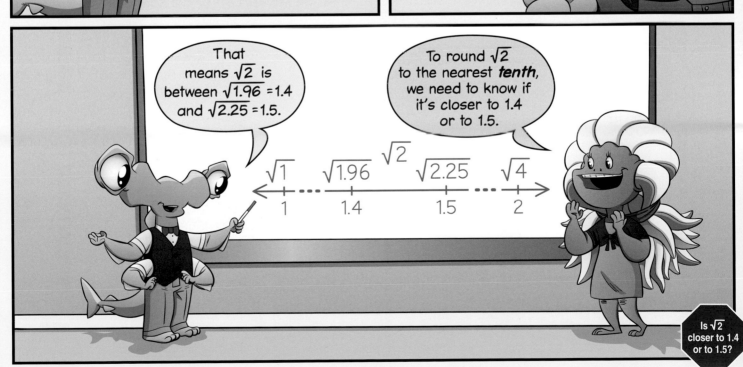

That means √2 is between √1.96 = 1.4 and √2.25 = 1.5.

To round √2 to the nearest *tenth*, we need to know if it's closer to 1.4 or to 1.5.

Is √2 closer to 1.4 or to 1.5?

To find out, we can compare $\sqrt{2}$ to 1.45.

Since $1.45^2 = 2.1025$, $1.45 = \sqrt{2.1025}$.

So, $\sqrt{2}$ is less than $\sqrt{2.1025} = 1.45$.

That means $\sqrt{2}$ is closer to 1.4 than to 1.5.

To the nearest tenth, $\sqrt{2}$ is about 1.4.

$$\sqrt{2} \approx 1.4$$

Nice job. We can also estimate and compare expressions that include square roots.

For example, which is greater: 7, or 5 times the square root of 2?

Which is greater:

$$7 \text{ or } 5\sqrt{2}?$$

$5\sqrt{2}$ MEANS $5 \cdot \sqrt{2}$ AND IS READ "FIVE ROOT TWO."
IN THE PRODUCT OF A NUMBER AND A SQUARE ROOT, WE PUT THE NUMBER LEFT OF THE SQUARE ROOT.

We just figured out that $\sqrt{2}$ is a little larger than 1.4.

So, $5\sqrt{2}$ is a little larger than $5 \cdot 1.4 = 7$.

I think I see a way to compare 7 to $5\sqrt{2}$ without estimating $\sqrt{2}$.

We can compare their squares.

$$7 < 5\sqrt{2}$$

Square 7 and $5\sqrt{2}$.

52

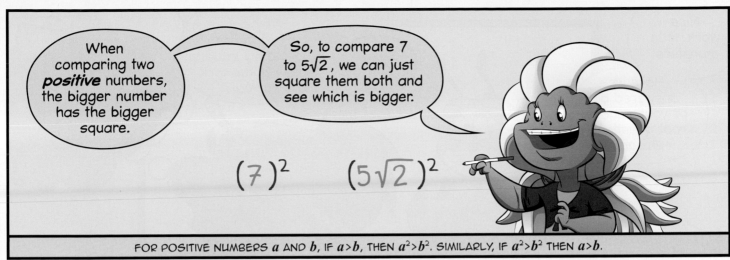

When comparing two **positive** numbers, the bigger number has the bigger square.

So, to compare 7 to $5\sqrt{2}$, we can just square them both and see which is bigger.

$$(7)^2 \qquad (5\sqrt{2})^2$$

FOR POSITIVE NUMBERS a AND b, IF $a > b$, THEN $a^2 > b^2$. SIMILARLY, IF $a^2 > b^2$ THEN $a > b$.

$7^2 = 49$.

$(5\sqrt{2})^2$ is $5\sqrt{2} \cdot 5\sqrt{2}$. How do we compute that?

$$(7)^2 \qquad (5\sqrt{2})^2$$
$$= 49 \qquad = 5\sqrt{2} \cdot 5\sqrt{2}$$

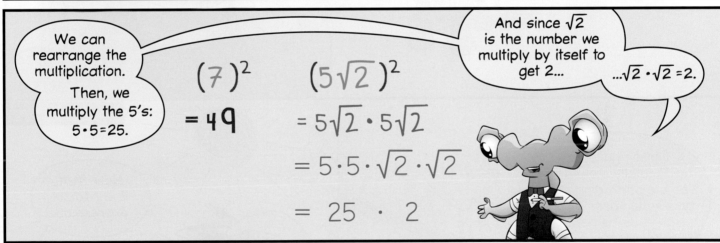

We can rearrange the multiplication. Then, we multiply the 5's: $5 \cdot 5 = 25$.

And since $\sqrt{2}$ is the number we multiply by itself to get 2...

...$\sqrt{2} \cdot \sqrt{2} = 2$.

$$(7)^2 \qquad (5\sqrt{2})^2$$
$$= 49 \qquad = 5\sqrt{2} \cdot 5\sqrt{2}$$
$$= 5 \cdot 5 \cdot \sqrt{2} \cdot \sqrt{2}$$
$$= 25 \cdot 2$$

So, $(5\sqrt{2})^2$ is 50!

And 50 is more than 49.

Yep. So, $5\sqrt{2}$ is greater than 7.

$$(7)^2 < (5\sqrt{2})^2$$
$$= 49 \qquad = 5\sqrt{2} \cdot 5\sqrt{2}$$
$$= 5 \cdot 5 \cdot \sqrt{2} \cdot \sqrt{2}$$
$$= 25 \cdot 2$$
$$= 50$$

Practice: Pages 37-45

RECESS

More or Less

More or Less is a card game for 2 players which uses two game boards, a $>$ marker, and 20 cards from a standard deck (Ace through 5 in all four suits; Aces count as 1's). The goal is to be the first player to play all the cards in your hand.

Setup

Each player begins with a square root game board and is dealt 5 cards from the shuffled deck. The remaining cards are placed in a draw pile as shown. You may print game boards at BeastAcademy.com, or make your own.

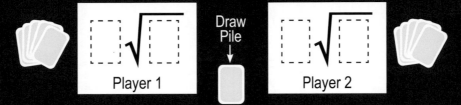

Beginning

Player 1 places two cards from their hand on the dashed rectangles of their game board to create an expression. Player 2 then places two cards from their hand on their game board to create an expression that is not equal to Player 1's. Players place a marker between the expressions to show which number is greater, pointing $>$ or $<$. For example, in the game below, we compare $3\sqrt{3}$ to $5\sqrt{1}$ by comparing their squares. Since $(3\sqrt{3})^2=27$, and $(5\sqrt{1})^2=25$, we have $3\sqrt{3} > 5\sqrt{1}$.

Play

Players take turns, starting with Player 1. On each turn, a player draws one card from the draw pile, then places 1 or 2 cards on their game board so that the relationship between the two expressions ($<$ or $>$) does not change. In the example above, Player 1 must create an expression that is greater than $5\sqrt{1}$. For example, Player 1 could use a 4 and a 2 to play $4\sqrt{2}$, since $4\sqrt{2}>5\sqrt{1}$. Or, Player 1 could simply place a 5 on top of either 3 to create $5\sqrt{3}$ or $3\sqrt{5}$, since both are greater than $5\sqrt{1}$.

If a Player creates an expression that does not work, they must pick up the cards played and forfeit their turn.

If a Player cannot create an expression that works, they must pass, and play continues with the other player.

Winning

The first player to play all of their cards wins. If neither player can play and the draw pile is empty, the game ends in a draw.

Variations

You may add additional digit cards in the deck (like 6's or 7's), or change the number of cards dealt to begin the game.

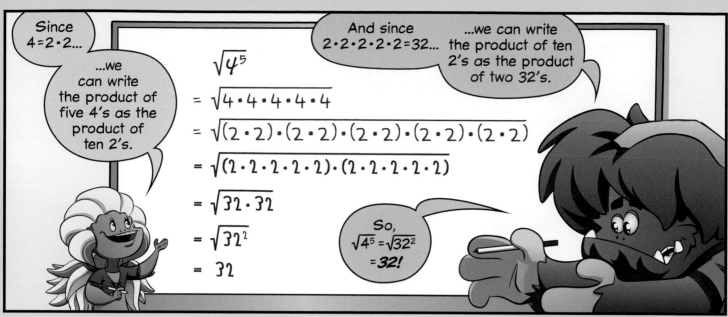

Since 4=2·2...

...we can write the product of five 4's as the product of ten 2's.

And since 2·2·2·2·2=32...

...we can write the product of ten 2's as the product of two 32's.

$$\sqrt{4^5}$$
$$= \sqrt{4 \cdot 4 \cdot 4 \cdot 4 \cdot 4}$$
$$= \sqrt{(2 \cdot 2) \cdot (2 \cdot 2) \cdot (2 \cdot 2) \cdot (2 \cdot 2) \cdot (2 \cdot 2)}$$
$$= \sqrt{(2 \cdot 2 \cdot 2 \cdot 2 \cdot 2) \cdot (2 \cdot 2 \cdot 2 \cdot 2 \cdot 2)}$$
$$= \sqrt{32 \cdot 32}$$
$$= \sqrt{32^2}$$
$$= 32$$

So, $\sqrt{4^5} = \sqrt{32^2} = 32!$

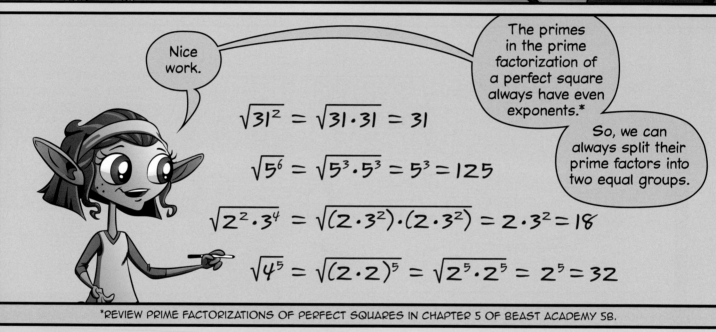

Nice work.

The primes in the prime factorization of a perfect square always have even exponents.*

So, we can always split their prime factors into two equal groups.

$$\sqrt{31^2} = \sqrt{31 \cdot 31} = 31$$

$$\sqrt{5^6} = \sqrt{5^3 \cdot 5^3} = 5^3 = 125$$

$$\sqrt{2^2 \cdot 3^4} = \sqrt{(2 \cdot 3^2) \cdot (2 \cdot 3^2)} = 2 \cdot 3^2 = 18$$

$$\sqrt{4^5} = \sqrt{(2 \cdot 2)^5} = \sqrt{2^5 \cdot 2^5} = 2^5 = 32$$

*REVIEW PRIME FACTORIZATIONS OF PERFECT SQUARES IN CHAPTER 5 OF BEAST ACADEMY 5B.

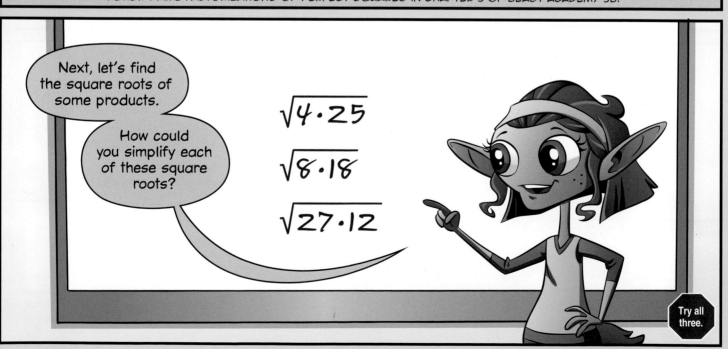

Next, let's find the square roots of some products.

How could you simplify each of these square roots?

$$\sqrt{4 \cdot 25}$$

$$\sqrt{8 \cdot 18}$$

$$\sqrt{27 \cdot 12}$$

Try all three.

58

$$\sqrt{4 \cdot 25} = \sqrt{100}$$
$$= 10$$

Since 4·25=100, $\sqrt{4 \cdot 25} = \sqrt{100}$ =10.

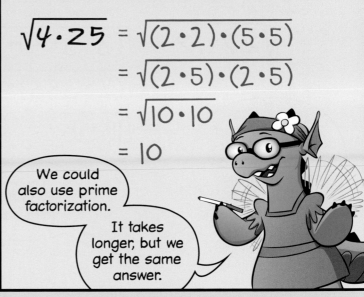

$$\sqrt{4 \cdot 25} = \sqrt{(2 \cdot 2) \cdot (5 \cdot 5)}$$
$$= \sqrt{(2 \cdot 5) \cdot (2 \cdot 5)}$$
$$= \sqrt{10 \cdot 10}$$
$$= 10$$

We could also use prime factorization.

It takes longer, but we get the same answer.

$$\sqrt{8 \cdot 18} = \sqrt{144}$$
$$= 12$$

Since 8·18=144, $\sqrt{8 \cdot 18} = \sqrt{144}$ =12.

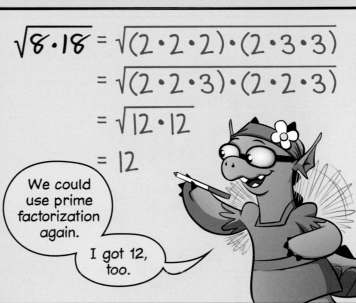

$$\sqrt{8 \cdot 18} = \sqrt{(2 \cdot 2 \cdot 2) \cdot (2 \cdot 3 \cdot 3)}$$
$$= \sqrt{(2 \cdot 2 \cdot 3) \cdot (2 \cdot 2 \cdot 3)}$$
$$= \sqrt{12 \cdot 12}$$
$$= 12$$

We could use prime factorization again.

I got 12, too.

This one's harder. 27·12 is 324.

So, $\sqrt{27 \cdot 12}$ =$\sqrt{324}$.

But, what's the square root of 324?

It's less than $\sqrt{400}$, which is 20.

Got it! I used prime factorization again.

$$\sqrt{27 \cdot 12} = \sqrt{324}$$

Compute $\sqrt{27 \cdot 12}$.

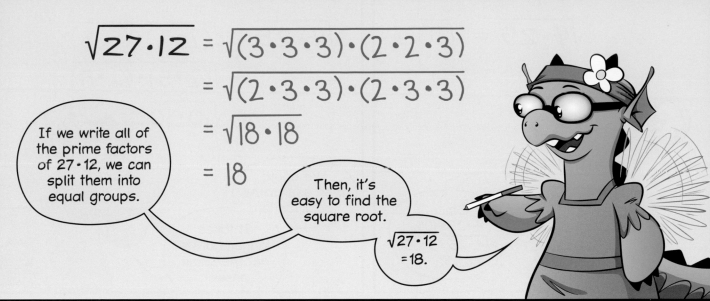

$$\sqrt{27 \cdot 12} = \sqrt{(3 \cdot 3 \cdot 3) \cdot (2 \cdot 2 \cdot 3)}$$
$$= \sqrt{(2 \cdot 3 \cdot 3) \cdot (2 \cdot 3 \cdot 3)}$$
$$= \sqrt{18 \cdot 18}$$
$$= 18$$

If we write all of the prime factors of 27 · 12, we can split them into equal groups.

Then, it's easy to find the square root.

$\sqrt{27 \cdot 12} = 18.$

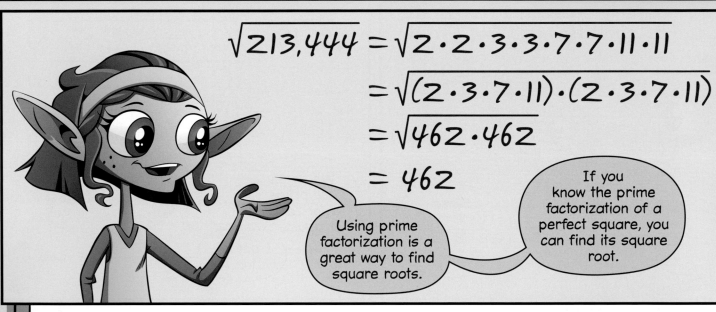

$$\sqrt{213{,}444} = \sqrt{2 \cdot 2 \cdot 3 \cdot 3 \cdot 7 \cdot 7 \cdot 11 \cdot 11}$$
$$= \sqrt{(2 \cdot 3 \cdot 7 \cdot 11) \cdot (2 \cdot 3 \cdot 7 \cdot 11)}$$
$$= \sqrt{462 \cdot 462}$$
$$= 462$$

Using prime factorization is a great way to find square roots.

If you know the prime factorization of a perfect square, you can find its square root.

Let's finish by finding the square roots of some fractions.

$$\sqrt{\frac{16}{25}} \qquad \sqrt{\frac{4}{64}}$$

$$\sqrt{\frac{18}{32}} \qquad \sqrt{\frac{14}{27} \cdot \frac{56}{75}}$$

Try all four.

The numerator and denominator of $\frac{16}{25}$ are both perfect squares. $16 = 4 \cdot 4$, and $25 = 5 \cdot 5$.

$$\sqrt{\frac{16}{25}} = \sqrt{\frac{4 \cdot 4}{5 \cdot 5}}$$

$$= \sqrt{\frac{4}{5} \cdot \frac{4}{5}}$$

$$= \frac{4}{5}$$

So, $\sqrt{\frac{16}{25}} = \frac{4}{5}$.

$$\sqrt{\frac{4}{64}} = \sqrt{\frac{2}{8} \cdot \frac{2}{8}}$$

$$= \frac{2}{8}$$

$$= \frac{1}{4}$$

Since $\sqrt{\frac{4}{64}} = \sqrt{\frac{2}{8} \cdot \frac{2}{8}}$, we know $\sqrt{\frac{4}{64}} = \frac{2}{8}$.

We can simplify $\frac{2}{8}$ to $\frac{1}{4}$.

$$\sqrt{\frac{4}{64}} = \sqrt{\frac{1}{16}}$$

$$= \sqrt{\frac{1}{4} \cdot \frac{1}{4}}$$

$$= \frac{1}{4}$$

I simplified *before* finding the square root. $\frac{4}{64}$ simplifies to $\frac{1}{16}$.

And since $\sqrt{\frac{1}{16}} = \sqrt{\frac{1}{4} \cdot \frac{1}{4}}$, we know $\sqrt{\frac{1}{16}} = \frac{1}{4}$.

We can simplify $\frac{18}{32}$ first to find $\sqrt{\frac{18}{32}}$. $\frac{18}{32}$ simplifies to $\frac{9}{16}$.

And since $\frac{9}{16} = \frac{3}{4} \cdot \frac{3}{4}$, we know $\sqrt{\frac{9}{16}} = \frac{3}{4}$.

$$\sqrt{\frac{18}{32}} = \sqrt{\frac{9}{16}}$$

$$= \frac{3}{4}$$

This last one is tough.

$$\sqrt{\frac{14}{27} \cdot \frac{56}{75}}$$

It's a product of two fractions, and neither of the fractions can be simplified.

Find the square root.

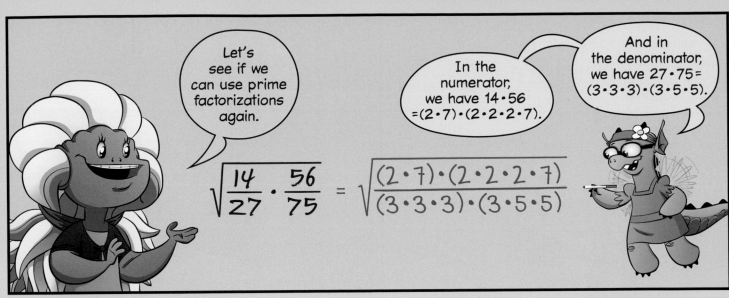

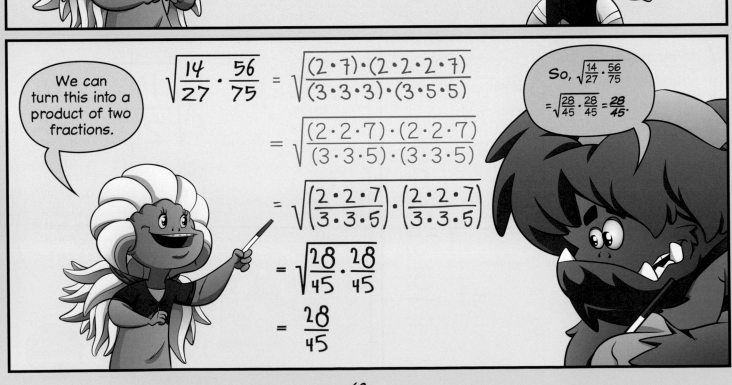

Practice: Pages 46-49

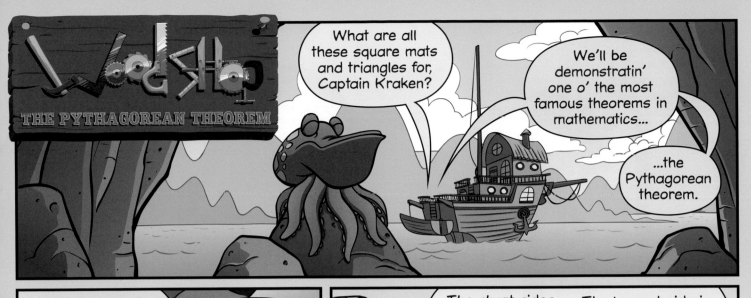

THE PYTHAGOREAN THEOREM

What are all these square mats and triangles for, Captain Kraken?

We'll be demonstratin' one o' the most famous theorems in mathematics...

...the Pythagorean theorem.

First, be sure that the side length o' the square mat be equal to the sum o' the two shortest sides of your triangle.

How can we tell which sides are the shortest?

The short sides of a right triangle meet at the right angle. They're called the *legs* of the triangle.

The longest side is across from the right angle. It's called the *hypotenuse*.

hypotenuse

legs

Squawk. Hi-pot-en-oose.

PRINT AND CUT YOUR OWN SQUARES AND TRIANGLES FOR THIS ACTIVITY AT BEASTACADEMY.COM.

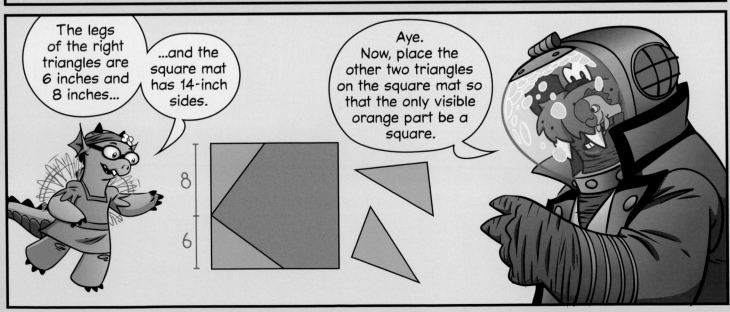

The legs of the right triangles are 6 inches and 8 inches...

...and the square mat has 14-inch sides.

8

6

Aye. Now, place the other two triangles on the square mat so that the only visible orange part be a square.

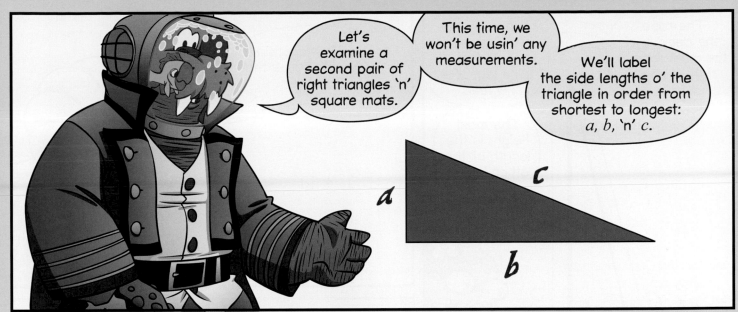

Let's examine a second pair of right triangles 'n' square mats.

This time, we won't be usin' any measurements.

We'll label the side lengths o' the triangle in order from shortest to longest: *a*, *b*, 'n' *c*.

We can arrange copies o' the triangle on square mats like we did before to make three yellow squares.

The side lengths of the yellow squares are *a*, *b*, and *c*...

...so the areas of the squares are a^2, b^2, and c^2.

b^2

c^2

a^2

$$a^2 + b^2 = c^2$$

And since the total area of the two small yellow squares equals the area of the big yellow square, $a^2 + b^2 = c^2$.

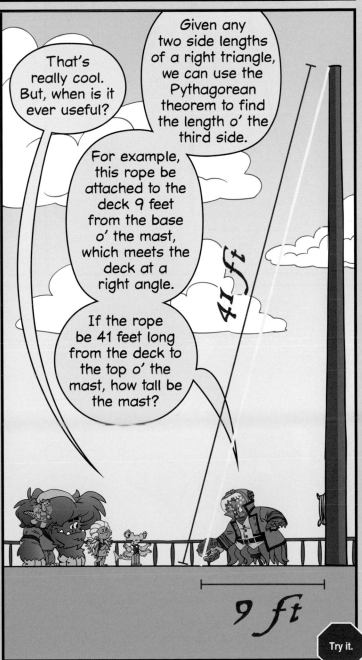

That's really cool. But, when is it ever useful?

Given any two side lengths of a right triangle, we can use the Pythagorean theorem to find the length o' the third side.

For example, this rope be attached to the deck 9 feet from the base o' the mast, which meets the deck at a right angle.

If the rope be 41 feet long from the deck to the top o' the mast, how tall be the mast?

41 ft

9 ft

Try it.

The rope, the deck, and the mast form a right triangle.

We know the hypotenuse, c, is 41 feet. One leg, a, is 9 feet.

The mast height is the length of the other leg, b.

$c = 41 \, ft$

b

$a = 9 \, ft$

The Pythagorean theorem tells us that $9^2 + b^2 = 41^2$.

$$9^2 + b^2 = 41^2$$

9^2 is 81, and 41^2 is 1,681. So, $81 + b^2 = 1,681$.

We can subtract 81 from both sides to get $b^2 = 1,600$.

$$9^2 + b^2 = 41^2$$
$$81 + b^2 = 1,681$$
$$\underline{-81 \qquad\qquad -81}$$
$$b^2 = 1,600$$

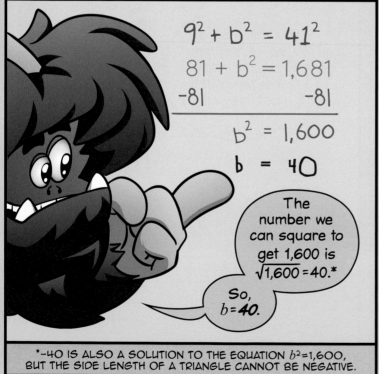

$$9^2 + b^2 = 41^2$$
$$81 + b^2 = 1,681$$
$$\underline{-81 \qquad\qquad -81}$$
$$b^2 = 1,600$$
$$b = 40$$

The number we can square to get 1,600 is $\sqrt{1,600} = 40$.*

So, $b = 40$.

*−40 IS ALSO A SOLUTION TO THE EQUATION $b^2 = 1,600$, BUT THE SIDE LENGTH OF A TRIANGLE CANNOT BE NEGATIVE.

The mast is 40 feet tall.

Will the missing side length always be an integer?

$41 \, ft$

$40 \, ft$

$9 \, ft$

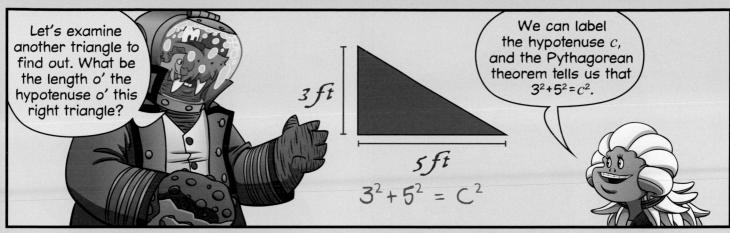

Let's examine another triangle to find out. What be the length o' the hypotenuse o' this right triangle?

We can label the hypotenuse c, and the Pythagorean theorem tells us that $3^2 + 5^2 = c^2$.

$3 ft$

$5 ft$

$3^2 + 5^2 = C^2$

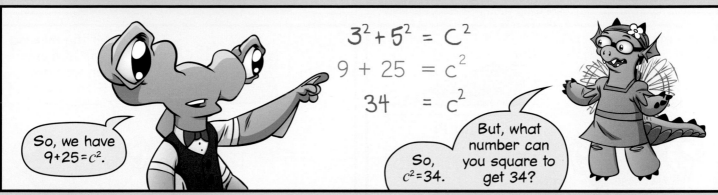

$$3^2 + 5^2 = C^2$$
$$9 + 25 = c^2$$
$$34 = c^2$$

So, we have $9 + 25 = c^2$.

So, $c^2 = 34$.

But, what number can you square to get 34?

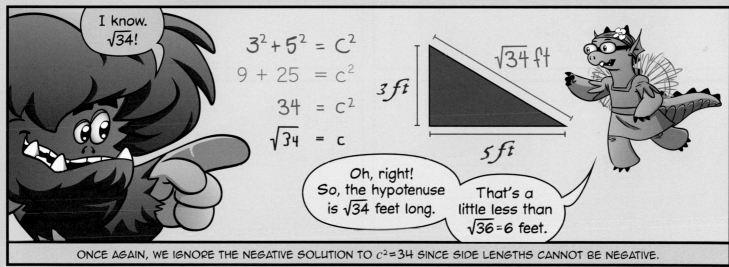

I know. $\sqrt{34}$!

$$3^2 + 5^2 = C^2$$
$$9 + 25 = c^2$$
$$34 = c^2$$
$$\sqrt{34} = c$$

$3 ft$

$\sqrt{34}\, ft$

$5 ft$

Oh, right! So, the hypotenuse is $\sqrt{34}$ feet long.

That's a little less than $\sqrt{36} = 6$ feet.

ONCE AGAIN, WE IGNORE THE NEGATIVE SOLUTION TO $c^2 = 34$ SINCE SIDE LENGTHS CANNOT BE NEGATIVE.

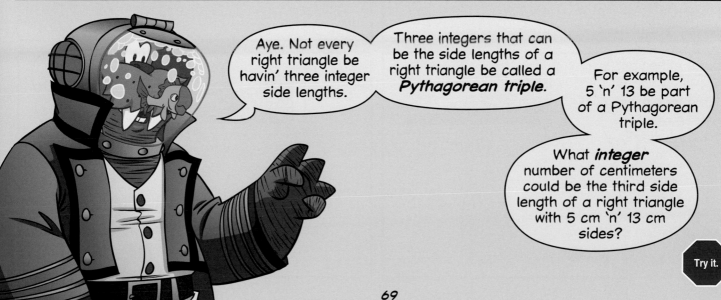

Aye. Not every right triangle be havin' three integer side lengths.

Three integers that can be the side lengths of a right triangle be called a **Pythagorean triple**.

For example, 5 'n' 13 be part of a Pythagorean triple.

What **integer** number of centimeters could be the third side length of a right triangle with 5 cm 'n' 13 cm sides?

Try it.

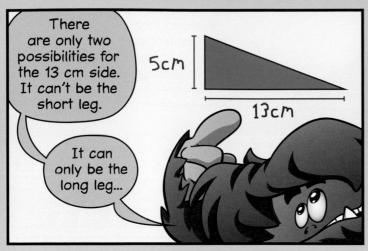

There are only two possibilities for the 13 cm side. It can't be the short leg.

It can only be the long leg...

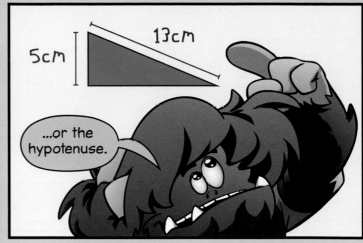

...or the hypotenuse.

If the missing length is the hypotenuse, then we have $5^2 + 13^2 = c^2$...

$$5^2 + 13^2 = c^2$$

...but if the missing length is a leg, then we have $5^2 + b^2 = 13^2$.

$$5^2 + b^2 = 13^2$$

So, either $c^2 = 194$...

$$5^2 + 13^2 = c^2$$
$$25 + 169 = c^2$$
$$194 = c^2$$

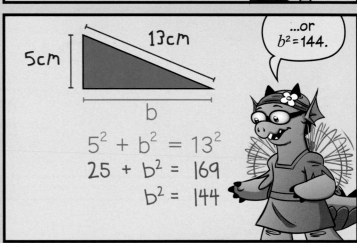

...or $b^2 = 144$.

$$5^2 + b^2 = 13^2$$
$$25 + b^2 = 169$$
$$b^2 = 144$$

So, we either get $c = \sqrt{194}$, which is a little less than $\sqrt{196} = 14$...

$$5^2 + 13^2 = c^2$$
$$25 + 169 = c^2$$
$$194 = c^2$$
$$\sqrt{194} = c$$

...or $b = \sqrt{144}$, which is 12.

$$5^2 + b^2 = 13^2$$
$$25 + b^2 = 169$$
$$b^2 = 144$$
$$b = 12$$

70

So, the only integer answer is 12 cm.

And since $5^2 + 12^2 = 13^2$, we know (5, 12, 13) is a Pythagorean triple.

$5^2 + 12^2 = 13^2$

Aye. (5, 12, 13) be a Pythagorean triple.

The best known Pythagorean triple be (3, 4, 5), since $3^2 + 4^2 = 5^2$.

$3^2 + 4^2 = 5^2$

MULTIPLYING ALL OF THE NUMBERS IN A PYTHAGOREAN TRIPLE BY THE SAME POSITIVE INTEGER GIVES ANOTHER PYTHAGOREAN TRIPLE. FOR EXAMPLE, DOUBLING (3,4,5) GIVES (6,8,10), AND $6^2 + 8^2 = 10^2$.

Here be a list o' the most common Pythagorean triples that could come up at the World Math Olympiad Championships.

We leave tomorrow!

Aye. Rosencrantz 'n' Guildenstern be preparin' the pneumatube for the trip.

$3^2 + 4^2 = 5^2$
$5^2 + 12^2 = 13^2$
$7^2 + 24^2 = 25^2$
$8^2 + 15^2 = 17^2$
$9^2 + 40^2 = 41^2$

71

Contents: Chapter 12

See page 64 in the Practice book for a recommended reading/practice sequence for Chapter 12.

Exponents 74
What power of 2 equals $2^8 \div 2^5$?

Negative Exponents 80
How could you write 3^{-2} as a fraction?

Pneumatube 84
How could you write 2^{20} as a power of 16?

The WMOC 90
Can you find the tensegrity structure?

Channel 5 92
What team won last year's World Math Olympiad Championship?

The Finals 93
Who will be crowned this year's champion?

Chapter 12:
Exponents

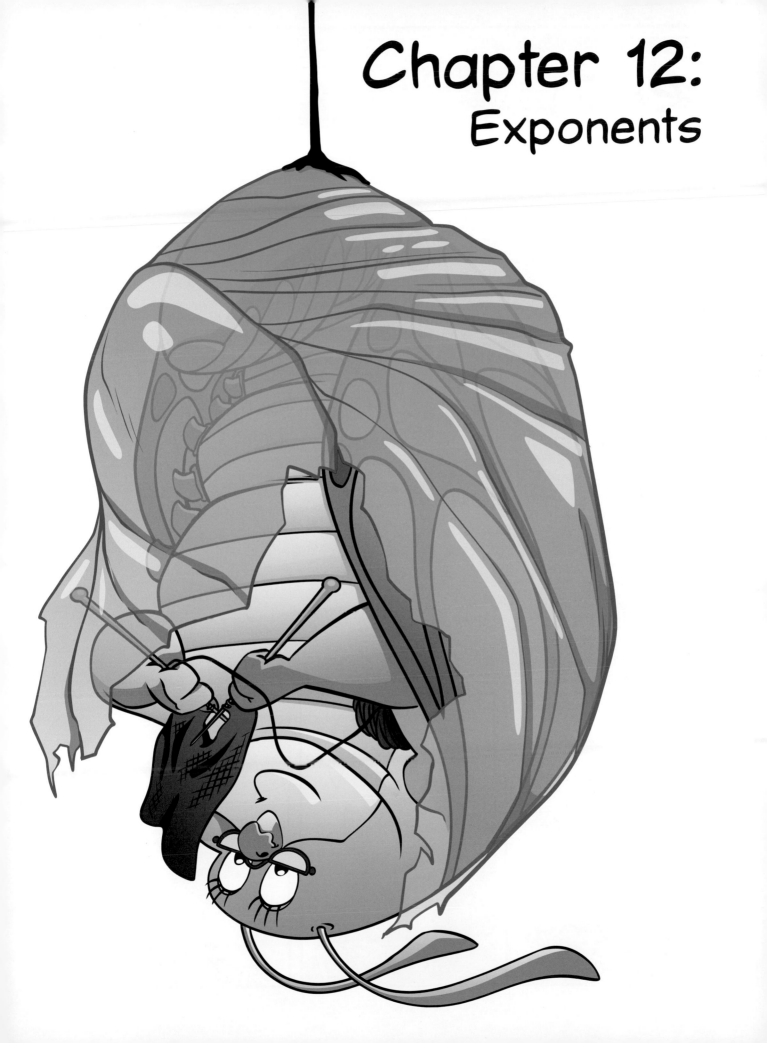

What are we prepping the pneumatube capsule for?

The math team is going to the World Math Olympiad!

Oh, right! Is that bushy-tailed kid still on the team?

Nope, he got invited to join the Star Search program.

The talent showcase TV show hosted by Ed McMonster where contestants compete for fame and fortune?

Nope, the space program dedicated to exploring neighboring star systems to discover extraterrestrial lifeforms.

Ohhh... *That* Star Search.

But, the nearest star outside our solar system is really, **really** far away.

Even if you could travel 100,000 miles per hour, it would take...

...a **really** long time.

Let's estimate how far you could travel in one year at 100,000 miles per hour.

Then, we can estimate how many years it would take to travel to the nearest star.

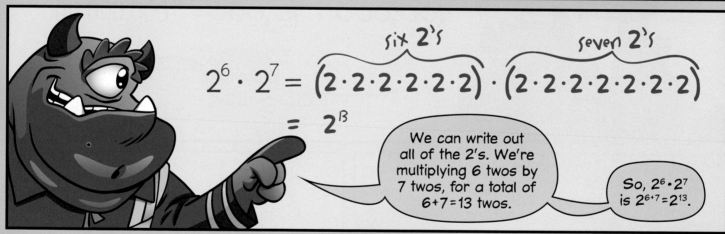
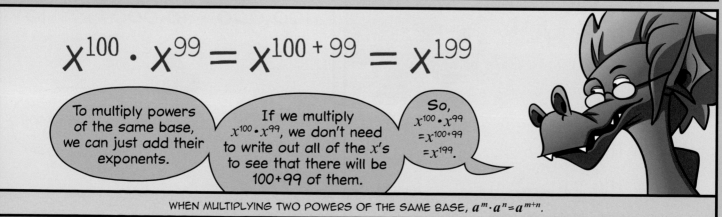

Exponents can be negative. Dividin' 7^4 by 7^9, we get 7^{-5}.

But, what does that even mean?

An exponent tells you how many copies of a number to multiply. How can you multiply **-5** copies of 7?

$$7^4 \div 7^9 = 7^{4-9} = 7^{-5}$$

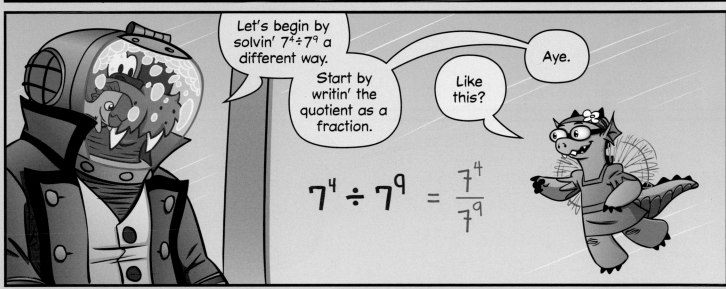

Let's begin by solvin' $7^4 \div 7^9$ a different way. Start by writin' the quotient as a fraction.

Like this?

Aye.

$$7^4 \div 7^9 = \frac{7^4}{7^9}$$

Since $7^4 \div 7^9 = 7^{-5}$, and $7^4 \div 7^9 = \frac{1}{7^5}$...

I see. Now, when we cancel 7's in the numerator and denominator, we're left with $\frac{1}{7^5}$.

...does that mean $7^{-5} = \frac{1}{7^5}$?

$$7^4 \div 7^9 = \frac{7^4}{7^9} = \frac{1}{7 \cdot 7 \cdot 7 \cdot 7 \cdot 7} = \frac{1}{7^5}$$

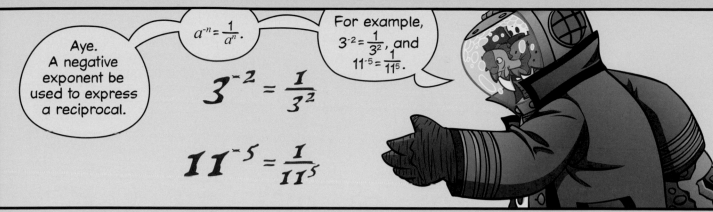

Aye. A negative exponent be used to express a reciprocal.

$a^{-n} = \frac{1}{a^n}$.

For example, $3^{-2} = \frac{1}{3^2}$, and $11^{-5} = \frac{1}{11^5}$.

$$3^{-2} = \frac{1}{3^2}$$

$$11^{-5} = \frac{1}{11^5}$$

Ok, I see.

Since exponents tell us how many copies of a number to multiply...

...to get the next-higher power of a number, we multiply by another copy of the number.

$5^4 = 625$ $\times 5$
$5^3 = 125$ $\times 5$
$5^2 = 25$ $\times 5$
$5^1 = 5$ $\times 5$

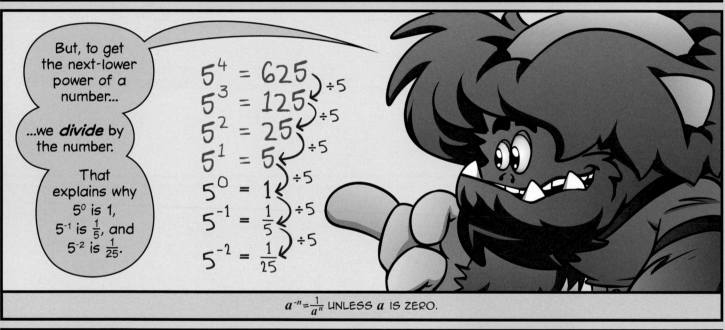

But, to get the next-lower power of a number...

...we *divide* by the number.

That explains why 5^0 is 1, 5^{-1} is $\frac{1}{5}$, and 5^{-2} is $\frac{1}{25}$.

$5^4 = 625$ $\div 5$
$5^3 = 125$ $\div 5$
$5^2 = 25$ $\div 5$
$5^1 = 5$ $\div 5$
$5^0 = 1$ $\div 5$
$5^{-1} = \frac{1}{5}$ $\div 5$
$5^{-2} = \frac{1}{25}$

$a^{-n} = \frac{1}{a^n}$ UNLESS a IS ZERO.

Do the multiplication and division rules for exponents work with negative exponents?

Try a few products 'n' quotients that include negative exponents.

$$5^{-2} \cdot 5^6$$

$$3^{-2} \cdot 3^{-5}$$

$$2^7 \div 2^{-4}$$

Try all three.

$$5^{-2} \cdot 5^6 = \frac{1}{5^2} \cdot 5^6$$
$$= \frac{5^6}{5^2}$$
$$= 5^{6-2}$$
$$= 5^4$$

Since $5^{-2} = \frac{1}{5^2}$, we can multiply $\frac{1}{5^2} \cdot 5^6$ to get 5^4.

$$5^{-2} \cdot 5^6 = 5^{(-2+6)}$$
$$= 5^4$$

That's the same answer we get when we add exponents!

$$3^{-2} \cdot 3^{-5} = \frac{1}{3^2} \cdot \frac{1}{3^5}$$
$$= \frac{1}{3^2 \cdot 3^5}$$
$$= \frac{1}{3^7}$$
$$= 3^{-7}$$

To multiply 3^{-2} by 3^{-5}, we can multiply $3^{-2} = \frac{1}{3^2}$ by $3^{-5} = \frac{1}{3^5}$.

$$3^{-2} \cdot 3^{-5} = 3^{-2+(-5)}$$
$$= 3^{-7}$$

Adding exponents gives us the same answer!

$$2^7 \div 2^{-4} = 2^7 \div \frac{1}{2^4}$$
$$= 2^7 \cdot \frac{2^4}{1}$$
$$= 2^{11}$$

To divide 2^7 by 2^{-4}, we can write 2^{-4} as $\frac{1}{2^4}$. To divide by $\frac{1}{2^4}$, we multiply by its reciprocal, $\frac{2^4}{1}$.

$$2^7 \div 2^{-4} = 2^{7-(-4)}$$
$$= 2^{7+4}$$
$$= 2^{11}$$

We get the same answer by subtracting exponents.

Excellent figurin'.

The rules for multiplyin' 'n' dividin' powers work whether the exponents be positive or negative.

We're at the terminal! Check it out!

Practice: Pages 65-77

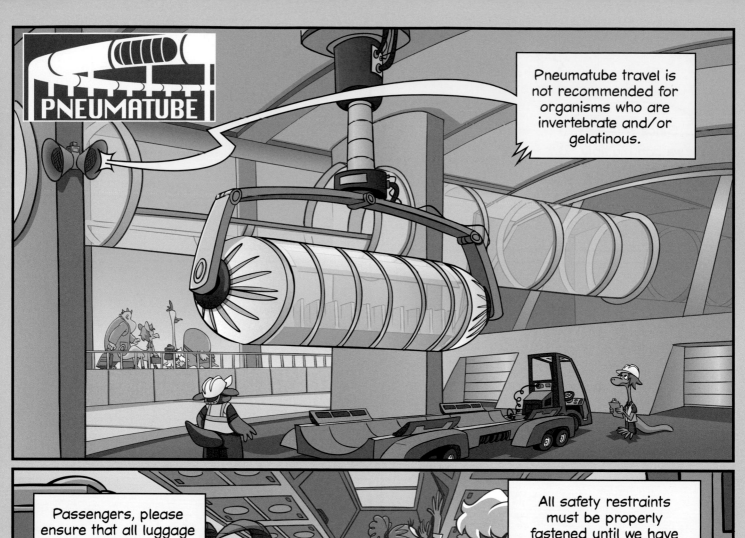

PNEUMATUBE

Pneumatube travel is not recommended for organisms who are invertebrate and/or gelatinous.

Passengers, please ensure that all luggage is properly stowed.

All safety restraints must be properly fastened until we have reached cruise velocity.

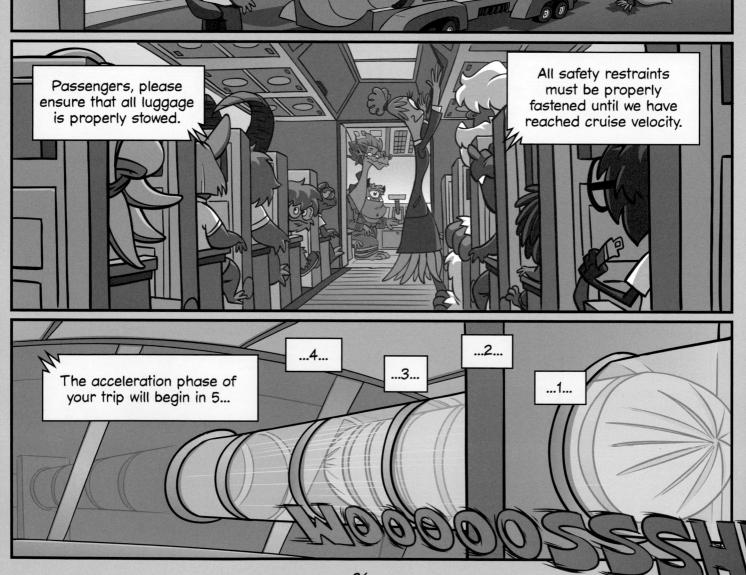

The acceleration phase of your trip will begin in 5...

...4...

...3...

...2...

...1...

WOOOOOSSSH

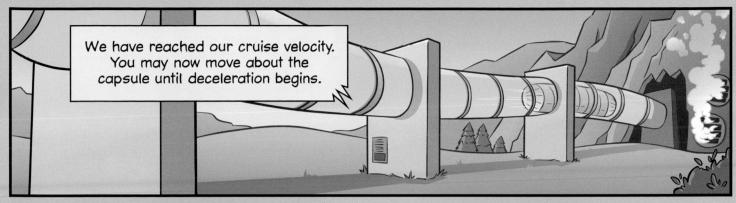

We have reached our cruise velocity. You may now move about the capsule until deceleration begins.

That was intense!

This year's Olympiad is halfway around the globe.

Pneumatube is the best way to get there fast.

Let's use our time wisely.

You've learned a few rules to help you compute with exponents.

Exponent Rules:

$$a^m \cdot a^n = a^{m+n}$$

$$a^m \div a^n = a^{m-n}$$

$$a^{-n} = \frac{1}{a^n}$$

DO NOT SIMPLY MEMORIZE THESE RULES. IF YOU UNDERSTAND WHY THEY WORK, REMEMBERING THEM IS EASY.

Try these three problems and see if you can find another rule to add to our list.

Express:

8^{24} as a power of 2

2^{20} as a power of 16

3^{12} as a power of $\frac{1}{27}$

Try all three.

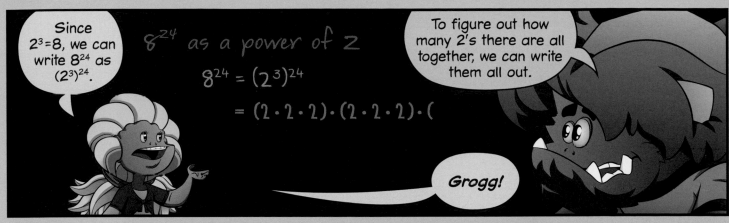

Since $2^3 = 8$, we can write 8^{24} as $(2^3)^{24}$.

8^{24} as a power of 2

$$8^{24} = (2^3)^{24}$$
$$= (2 \cdot 2 \cdot 2) \cdot (2 \cdot 2 \cdot 2) \cdot ($$

To figure out how many 2's there are all together, we can write them all out.

Grogg!

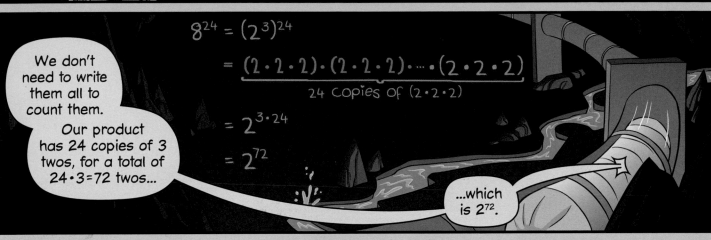

We don't need to write them all to count them.

Our product has 24 copies of 3 twos, for a total of $24 \cdot 3 = 72$ twos...

$$8^{24} = (2^3)^{24}$$
$$= \underbrace{(2 \cdot 2 \cdot 2) \cdot (2 \cdot 2 \cdot 2) \cdot \cdots \cdot (2 \cdot 2 \cdot 2)}_{24 \text{ copies of } (2 \cdot 2 \cdot 2)}$$
$$= 2^{3 \cdot 24}$$
$$= 2^{72}$$

...which is 2^{72}.

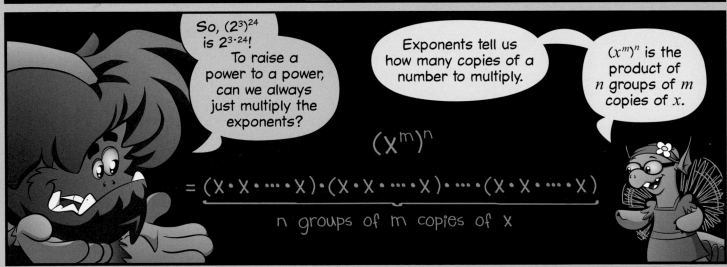

So, $(2^3)^{24}$ is $2^{3 \cdot 24}$! To raise a power to a power, can we always just multiply the exponents?

Exponents tell us how many copies of a number to multiply.

$(x^m)^n$ is the product of n groups of m copies of x.

$$(x^m)^n$$
$$= \underbrace{(x \cdot x \cdot \cdots \cdot x) \cdot (x \cdot x \cdot \cdots \cdot x) \cdot \cdots \cdot (x \cdot x \cdot \cdots \cdot x)}_{n \text{ groups of } m \text{ copies of } x}$$

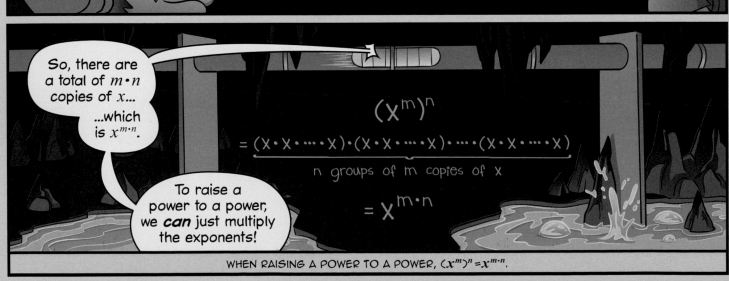

So, there are a total of $m \cdot n$ copies of x...

...which is $x^{m \cdot n}$.

To raise a power to a power, we **can** just multiply the exponents!

$$(x^m)^n$$
$$= \underbrace{(x \cdot x \cdot \cdots \cdot x) \cdot (x \cdot x \cdot \cdots \cdot x) \cdot \cdots \cdot (x \cdot x \cdot \cdots \cdot x)}_{n \text{ groups of } m \text{ copies of } x}$$
$$= x^{m \cdot n}$$

WHEN RAISING A POWER TO A POWER, $(x^m)^n = x^{m \cdot n}$.

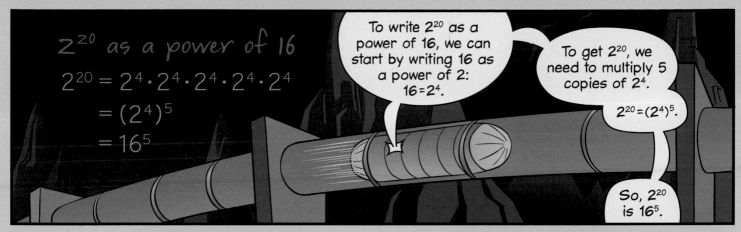
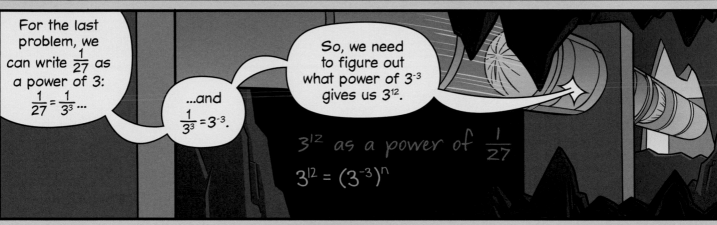

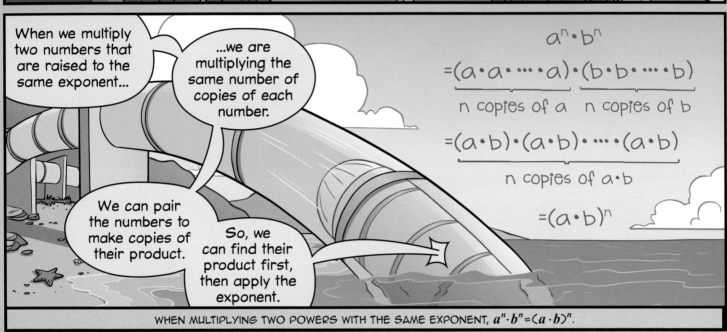

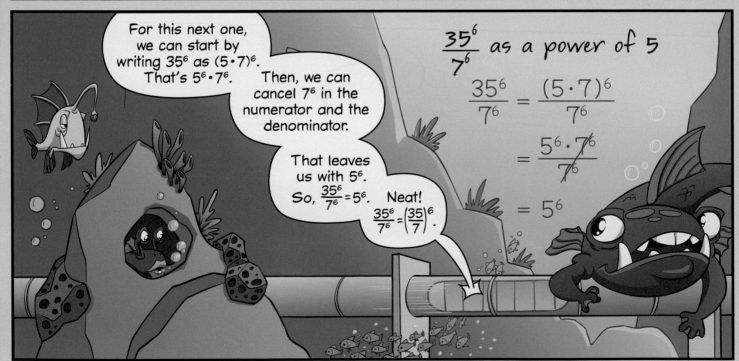

$$\frac{a^n}{b^n} = \frac{\overbrace{(a \cdot a \cdot \dots \cdot a)}^{n \text{ copies of } a}}{\underbrace{(b \cdot b \cdot \dots \cdot b)}_{n \text{ copies of } b}} = \underbrace{\frac{a}{b} \cdot \frac{a}{b} \cdot \dots \cdot \frac{a}{b}}_{n \text{ copies of } \frac{a}{b}} = \left(\frac{a}{b}\right)^n$$

When we divide two numbers that are raised to the same exponent...

...we are dividing the same number of copies of each number.

We can pair the numbers to make copies of their quotient.

So, we can divide the numbers first, then apply the exponent.

WHEN DIVIDING TWO POWERS WITH THE SAME EXPONENT, $\frac{a^n}{b^n} = \left(\frac{a}{b}\right)^n$, WHICH IS THE SAME AS $a^n \div b^n = (a \div b)^n$.

Well done!

Now, we have lots of rules you can apply when working with exponents. Understanding **why** each rule works is the best way to remember them all.

Exponent Rules:

$$a^m \cdot a^n = a^{m+n}$$
$$a^m \div a^n = a^{m-n}$$
$$a^{-n} = \frac{1}{a^n}$$
$$(a^m)^n = a^{m \cdot n}$$
$$a^n \cdot b^n = (a \cdot b)^n$$
$$a^n \div b^n = (a \div b)^n$$

Your attention, please.

Passengers must secure all loose items to prepare for deceleration.

Why is that a rule?

Oh, I see.

MATH TEAM
The WMOC

Wow!

Are all of these monsters here to watch **us**?

There are competitions for all levels and over a dozen different categories.

But, the competition is just one part of the World Math Olympiad Championships.

It's a huge event!

91

Practice: Pages 78-85

CHANNEL 5

We're back, coming to you live from the World Math Olympiad Championships.

We've just received results from the written contest for the elementary division, Mike.

No huge surprises, here.

Three of these teams are familiar to the WMOC stage.

Excel Elementary is here to defend their championship from last year...

...but few expected the team from Beast Academy to make the finals without phenom Max Norris.

PRESTIGE PREP

Prestige Prep makes the finals for the ninth year in a row, along with the Talent School team that finished fourth last year.

EXCEL ES

TALENT SCHOOL

BEAST ACADEMY

They must be thrilled with their written round performance, Phil.

Few teams could make the finals of the WMOC after the loss of a superstar like Max.

We're in for a treat, Mike.

Let's join the action live as the top four teams make their way on to the stage.

MATH TEAM
The Finals

Welcome, participants and spectators to our championship final in the elementary division.

Teams have been briefed on the rules. The first team to correctly answer 10 questions will be crowned champion. Teams, please test your buzzers before our first question.

boop!

bzzzt!

zeet!

ding!

Excellent! Let's begin.

Question 1: What is 0.032% of 5^5?

Try it.

REMEMBER, WHEN WE CANCEL A FACTOR THAT IS DIVIDED BY ITSELF, WE GET 1 (NOT 0). $\frac{2^5}{2^5 \cdot 5^5} \cdot 5^5 = \frac{2^5 \cdot 5^5}{2^5 \cdot 5^5} = 1$.

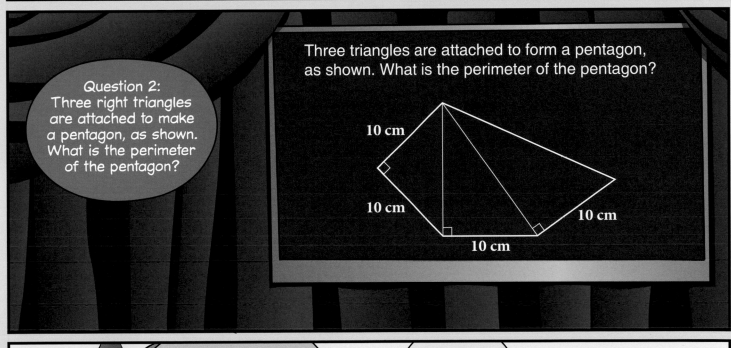

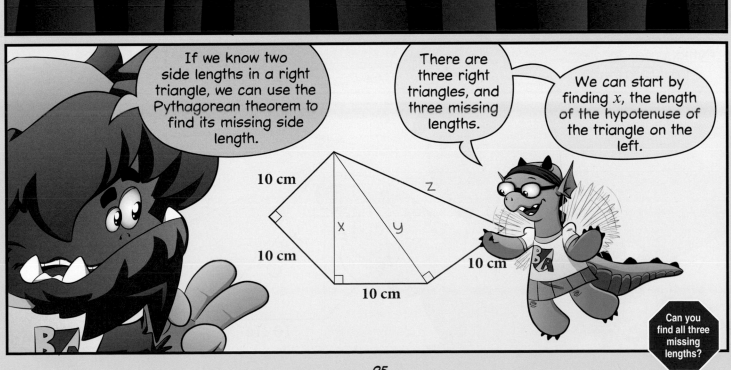

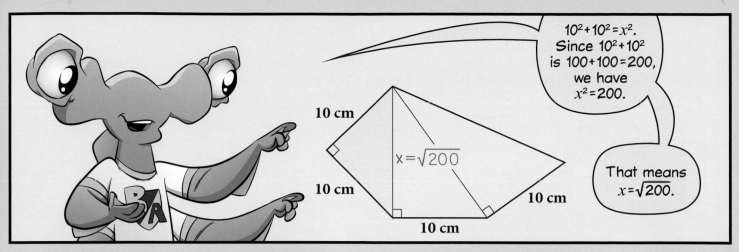

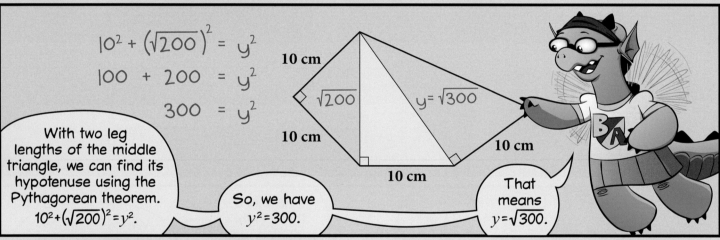

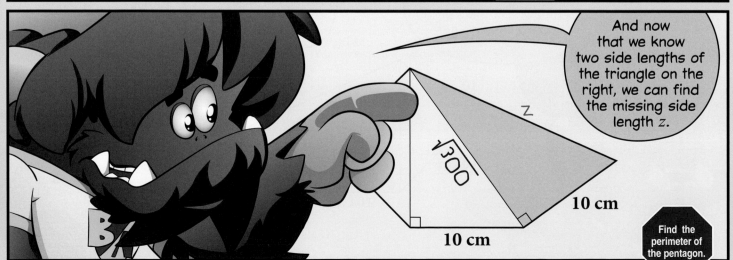

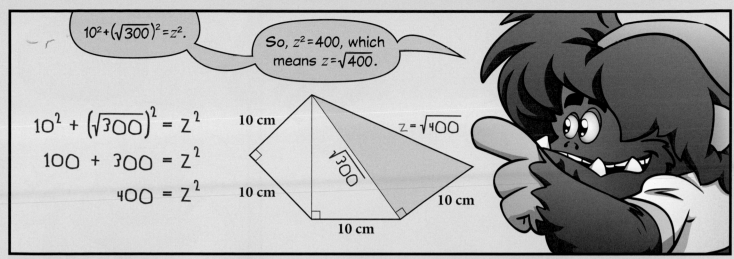

$$10^2 + \left(\sqrt{300}\right)^2 = z^2$$
$$100 + 300 = z^2$$
$$400 = z^2$$

$$\frac{2^{99} + 2^{98}}{2^{100}} = \frac{2^{98}(2+1)}{2^{98}(2^2)} = \frac{3}{4} = \frac{75}{100} =$$

ding!

75%.

Correct! Beast Academy scores a point.

Question 4: For how many positive integers x is $9^{45} < x^{30} < 8^{50}$?

How do we even begin?

9^{45} and 8^{50} are way too big to compute.

Does it help to write 9^{45} as $(3^2)^{45} = 3^{90}$ and 8^{50} as $(2^3)^{50} = 2^{150}$?

It might.

$$9^{45} < x^{30} < 8^{50}$$
$$(3^2)^{45} < x^{30} < (2^3)^{50}$$
$$3^{90} < x^{30} < 2^{150}$$

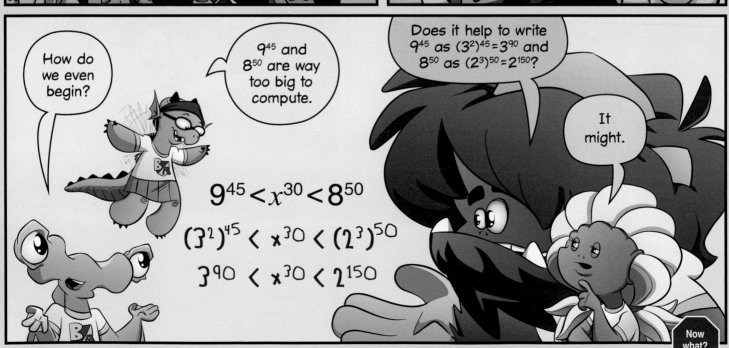

Now what?

I know! Since 90 and 150 are multiples of 30, we can write 3^{90} and 2^{150} as numbers to the 30th power!

$$9^{45} < x^{30} < 8^{50}$$
$$(3^2)^{45} < x^{30} < (2^3)^{50}$$
$$3^{90} < x^{30} < 2^{150}$$
$$(3^3)^{30} < x^{30} < (2^5)^{30}$$

3·30=90, so $(3^3)^{30}=3^{90}$.

And since 5·30=150, $(2^5)^{30}=2^{150}$.

That gives us $(3^3)^{30}<x^{30}<(2^5)^{30}$.

And since $3^3=27$ and $2^5=32$, we have $27^{30}<x^{30}<32^{30}$.

$$9^{45} < x^{30} < 8^{50}$$
$$(3^2)^{45} < x^{30} < (2^3)^{50}$$
$$3^{90} < x^{30} < 2^{150}$$
$$(3^3)^{30} < x^{30} < (2^5)^{30}$$
$$27^{30} < x^{30} < 32^{30}$$

Since the question asks for *positive* integers, x has to be between 27 and 32.

bzzzt! zeet!

Excel Elementary was first to ring in.

8.

Sorry, 8 is not correct.

Talent School rang in next.

4.

Correct! After four questions, the score is tied at 1 all.

THE INTEGERS ARE 28, 29, 30, AND 31. RAISING A NEGATIVE NUMBER TO AN EVEN POWER GIVES A POSITIVE RESULT, SO THERE ARE ALSO FOUR NEGATIVE INTEGERS FOR WHICH $27^{30}<x^{30}<32^{30}$: −28, −29, −30, AND −31.

Teams are returning to the stage.

Let's get back to the action!

Welcome back, competitors. Please take your positions and prepare for the next question.

Question 35: The square root of an integer n is between 9 and 10. The square root of $2n$ is between 14 and 15. What is n?

n has to be less than this...

...but n is greater than that...

So, n has to be...

What is n?

ding!

99.

Correct! Beast Academy scores their 9th point!

How did you guys...?

Numbers with a square root between 9 and 10 are between $9^2=81$ and $10^2=100$. So, n is between 81 and 100.

Numbers with a square root between 14 and 15 are between $14^2=196$ and $15^2=225$.

So, $2n$ is between 196 and 225, which means n is between 98 and 112.5.

So, n has to be more than 98, but less than 100.

Since n is an integer, it can only be 99.

Wow, nice teamwork!

How can a power of 3 equal 2?

Since $3^0 = 1$ and $3^1 = 3$, the exponent in the power of 3 must be between 0 and 1.

So, if $x-1$ is between 0 and 1, that means x is between 1 and 2.

$$3^0 = 1$$
$$3^{(x-1)} = 2$$
$$3^1 = 3$$

Maybe we don't need to find x to figure out what $9^{(x+1)}$ equals.

What do you mean, Grogg?

Maybe we can use exponent rules to make the expressions simpler.

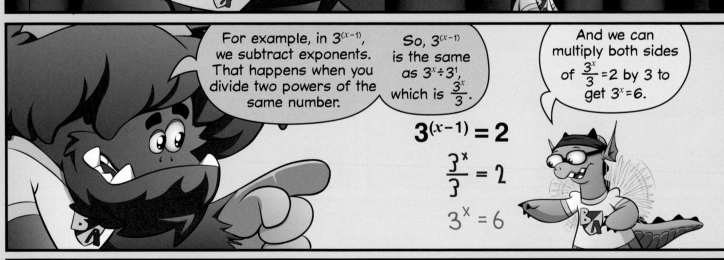

For example, in $3^{(x-1)}$, we subtract exponents. That happens when you divide two powers of the same number.

So, $3^{(x-1)}$ is the same as $3^x \div 3^1$, which is $\frac{3^x}{3}$.

And we can multiply both sides of $\frac{3^x}{3} = 2$ by 3 to get $3^x = 6$.

$$3^{(x-1)} = 2$$
$$\frac{3^x}{3} = 2$$
$$3^x = 6$$

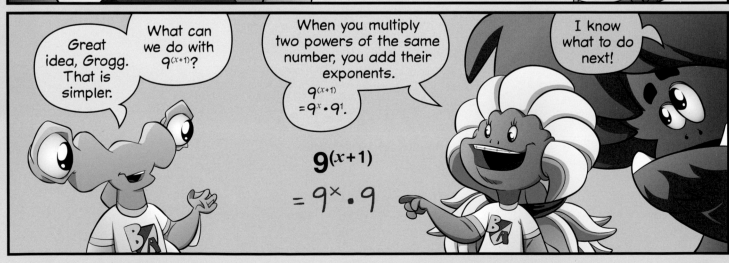

Great idea, Grogg. That is simpler.

What can we do with $9^{(x+1)}$?

When you multiply two powers of the same number, you add their exponents.

$$9^{(x+1)} = 9^x \cdot 9^1.$$

I know what to do next!

$$9^{(x+1)} = 9^x \cdot 9$$

107

Elizabeth Wyvern coached three Beast Academy teams to Beast Island championships before becoming a decorated professor at BA.

Alexander Gardner's investment aptitude earned him enough money to open his own theatre company, where he now directs and performs.

Groggorius George became the world's youngest Competibot champion. He now builds a variety of both extraordinary and practical robots.

And Wendolyn DeMonstre created her own robust programming language, which is now used around the world (and in all of Grogg's bots.)

108

Practice: Pages 86-91

Meanwhile, Fiona Fawn joined Max Norris on the Star Search program at Beast Island Tech, where they helped discover a distant blue planet they think *might* support intelligent life.

Index

Symbols

% symbol, 14

A

aliens, 74, 79

C

Calamitous Clod. See Clod, Calamitous
Channel 5, 92
chrysalis, 73
Clean Sweep, 28–31
Clod, Calamitous, 36
comparing square roots, 48–53, 55
cube root, 46
cubing a number, 46

D

decimal
    converting to a percent, 20–23

E

EnormousNoggins.com, 13, 18
estimating square roots, 48–53
Excel Elementary, 92, 94, 99–100, 103
exponent, 58, 73–109
    equations, 103–105
    in a product, 75–76
    in a quotient, 77–79, 80–81
    negative, 80–83
    rules, 85, 89, 104–105
    same (division), 88–89
    same (multiplication), 88
extraterrestrial lifeforms, 74, 79

F

Fiona. See Math Team
fraction
    comparing, 30
    converting to a percent, 16–18, 29–31
    of a number, 25

G

Grok. See Lab
Gym
    Percents & Decimals, 19–23

H

hippopotamoose, 34–35
hypotenuse, 64–70, 95–97

I

imaginary number, 44
index, 110

K

Kraken. See Woodshop

L

Lab
    Proportions, 33–39
Land Lobbers, 28–31
leg (of a right triangle), 64–70, 96

M

Math Team
    The Finals, 93–109
    The WMOC, 90–91
    Tricky Square Roots, 56–63
Max (Norris), 91–92, 109
Mike and Phil, 92, 100, 103, 105
Möbius Flip, 90
Ms. Q.
    Estimation, 48–54
    Percents & Fractions, 14–18

N

negative
    square root of, 43–44
negative exponents, 80–83
Notes
    Lizzie's, 47

P

percent, 13–39
    converting, 14–23
    converting to a decimal, 19–20, 22–23
    converting to a fraction, 15–18
    greater than 100%, 32
    mental computations, 25–27
    of a number, 24–27, 93–95
    proportions, 33–39
    symbol, 14

percentage, 29–30. See percent
perfect square, 42
pirate taxes, 24–27
Pneumatube, 71, 80–83, 84–89
porcupuma, 36
power
    dividing, 77–79, 80–81
    dividing (same exponent), 88–89
    multiplying, 75–76
    multiplying (same exponent), 88
    of 10, 75–78
    raised to a power, 86–87
Prestige Prep, 92, 97, 100, 103
prime factorization, 58–63
    of a perfect square, 58
proportions, 33–39
Pythagorean theorem, 64–71, 95–97
    proof, 67
Pythagorean triple, 69–71

R

radical expression, 54
radical (symbol), 54
ratio, 33, 38
rattlesnail, 36
Recess
    More or Less, 55
reciprocal, 82
R&G
    Exponents, 74–79
    Finding Percents, 28–32
    Square Roots, 42–46
Rote. See Gym

S

spiralac, 26
square root, 41–71, 101–102
    comparing, 48–54
    definition, 42–43
    estimation, 48–54
    of a decimal, 45–46
    of a fraction, 60–62
    of a negative number, 43–44
    of a product, 58–62

squaring
    a number that ends in 5, 47
    any two-digit number, 47
    finding the next square, 45
    square roots, 53–54
squidolphin, 33
Star Search, 74, 91, 109
SuaveShark.com, 14, 18

T

Talent School, 92, 99–100, 103
tensegrity structure, 72, 90

W

Woodshop
    Negative Exponents, 80–83
    Percent of a Number, 24–27
    The Pythagorean Theorem, 64–71
World Math Olympiad Championships,
    19, 56, 71, 74, 80, 90–107

Want more Beast Academy?
Try Beast Academy Online!

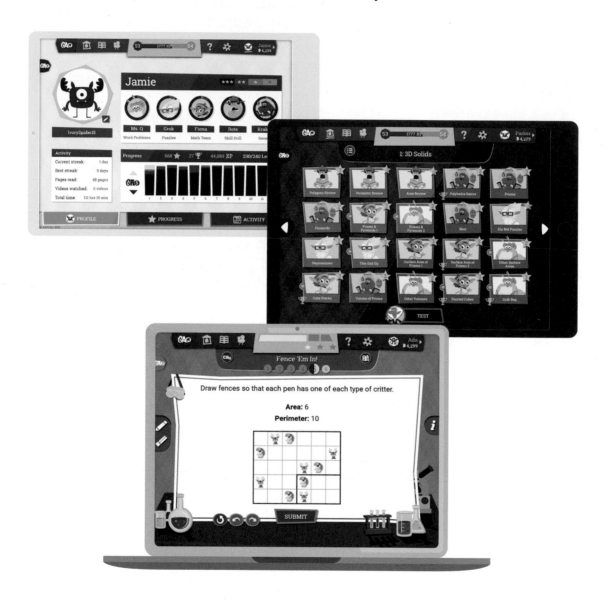

Learn more at BeastAcademy.com